Josie's Journal

by Emma Whitehorn ★ illustrated by Helen Endres

Harcourt

Orlando Boston Dallas Chicago San Diego

Visit *The Learning Site!*

www.harcourtschool.com

Wednesday, September 5—The first day of seventh grade

Maybe *finally* this is going to be a good year—maybe! I've made a New-School-Year Resolution: I am *not* going to feel left out—no way.

Right before school, Betsy Olsen, who's in eighth grade, came up and asked if I was interested in playing soccer on the Morrisville under-14 travel team—the Tigers. She said she really hoped I was because they always have too many forwards, and they need people to play midfield, which is my favorite position. Two other kids on the team are in my class, Carla Bernstein and Megan Rogers, and I like them—at least I think I do—so I guess I'm off to a good start on my resolution.

Awesome—more good news: I got the teacher I wanted, Mr. Spears. Everybody says he's really, really, really, exceptionally nice and also a great teacher. Even though he assigns a lot of homework, he lets you hand it in a day late if you have a reasonable excuse.

There's a new girl in our class, and Mr. Spears told us that she comes from China. He had her stand up while he introduced her; her name is Mei Mei Wu Qiau. I copied it down, but, of course, that was useless because I don't know how to pronounce it, and I can't ask her, because she doesn't speak English yet; all I know is her first name is pronounced *May May*—as in the month of May. Mr. Spears kept repeating things for Mei Mei; when he passed out our math textbooks, he said very, very slowly, "This is for mathematics."

She gave him a teeny tiny nod and said something nobody could hear; she's so shy and small that she seems totally lost. At least she's lucky (me too!) to get Mr. Spears for a teacher because he always tries to help out kids who are having a rough time, and I could tell that he was taking her under his wing.

We got out at noon today, and Megan and Carla invited me to walk to the bus with them. I was in a fantastically good mood, and I gave Mei Mei a smile as I was leaving; I was probably the only person in my class who did even that much. Everybody else seemed sort of paralyzed, too scared to even try.

Thursday, September 6

When I was stuffing all my soccer paraphernalia into my locker this morning, I noticed Mei Mei was putting something in her locker, just two down from mine. She gave me this tentative look of recognition, as if to say, *Do you remember me? Will you talk to me today?*

I don't know why I did this, but instead of acknowledging her, I turned and started arranging and rearranging everything in

my locker, and I didn't look over at her again, but afterward I felt bad for not making an effort.

At lunch time, the twins, Katy and Allison, sat with Mei Mei and tried to have a conversation; I was sitting at the same table and I heard them say, "How's it going?" and "Is our school like your old school?" You could tell Mei Mei was totally mystified. She shook her head in confusion, and pretty soon Katy and Allison stopped trying; instead they concentrated on their yogurt, tortilla chips, granola bars, and chocolate milk.

Mei Mei had brought chopsticks and a plastic margarine container of rice and some dark sauce she sprinkled on it, and she was drinking tea out of a glass jar with a screw top.

"What's that she's eating?" I heard Brad Monahan mutter under his breath to Michael Dunfey. Then he and Michael immediately began horsing around, shoving their sandwiches at each other and kicking their chairs back until Mr. Spears came over and made them stop.

For the rest of the day, I had this funny feeling that I hadn't been all that nice to Mei Mei, even though I hadn't been mean. I hadn't done anything to her, but I hadn't made any effort to help her, either.

After school, I walked to the bus again with Megan and Carla, and I realized that the three of us were all getting to be friends. It's great to have some new friends and *not* feel left out for a change; I guess my New-School-Year Resolution is working—kind of.

Friday, September 7

Tonight at dinner, my parents told me that Mei Mei lives one block over from us in an enormous tan-brick apartment building. They explained that they know this because the Thompsons—our friends—are sponsoring Mei Mei's family in the United States. Then Dad raised his eyebrows at Mom, and Mom cleared her throat in a funny way that told me they were about to give me some bad news. I was right: they admitted that they had volunteered me to walk home with Mei Mei, starting this Monday. They said that the Thompsons had already told Mei Mei's family—so it was a done deal, no way out for me. Talk about putting a person on the spot. When I started to complain,

Mom told me to stop, because I wasn't the only one helping out Mei Mei's family; Mom had volunteered to take Mei Mei's mother grocery shopping.

"OK," I said, "I'll do it for now, but once soccer starts, the Thompsons are going to have to find another kid to help."

Monday, September 10

I was nervous about whether Mei Mei really expected to walk home with me today, so I asked Mr. Spears in private for some help. "Try asking her yourself," he suggested.

I sat next to her at lunch, and I said, "I'm going to walk home with you after school today," and Mei Mei looked into my eyes as if she were hoping she could find a translation there. "Home—*today*," I repeated, and when she nodded, her silky black hair flew around her cheeks.

"Mei Mei understands a lot," Mr. Spears told me just before dismissing us. "When people learn a foreign language, their aural comprehension is usually way ahead of their capacity to speak in the language."

"Their what-all comprehension?" I asked.

"Aural—*a-u-r-a-l*—what they hear. Kids catch on quickly, you know, especially when they have a supportive friend," he said, smiling at me. Then he saw Megan and Carla coming toward me, and he added, "or several supportive friends."

The four of us walked out together, but it was Megan and Carla ahead and Mei Mei and me behind. They climbed on the bus first and took seats beside each other; so much for my New-School-Year Resolution. As Mei Mei and I crowded past them, Megan looked up and said, "Soccer starts tomorrow. Sure hope you can make it—*Josie.*"

She never mentioned Mei Mei's name.

After Mei Mei and I got off the bus, I tried to think of ways to begin a conversation as we walked along, but it was hard, and Mei Mei kept looking at me nervously, as if she was afraid she'd offended me by not being able to speak better English.

We went up a narrow stairwell to the second floor of her building, and her mother answered the door a second after Mei Mei rang. Mei Mei's mother spoke rapidly to Mei Mei, meanwhile nodding appreciatively to me. Finally she gestured for us both to come in. There was one long, tattered-looking sofa in the living room, two plastic yard chairs, and no rugs, although the tile floor was gleaming clean. A very old, very small woman was sitting on the sofa.

Mei Mei's mother said "grandmother" to me and bowed toward the older woman, so I figured that I was being introduced. I boomed out with all the politeness I could muster, "My name is Josie and I'm very pleased to meet you," but my voice was way too loud, and hearing myself made me embarrassed.

Mei Mei's grandmother gave me the slightest nod anyone could possibly give and stared steadily at me, as if she was thinking something like—*Mei Mei, this new friend of yours isn't as nice as she's pretending to be.*

Of course, Mei Mei's grandmother wasn't really thinking that. I'm not sure why I was ashamed of myself, though, for not wanting to be there to help Mei Mei. They kept chattering and smiling at me.

Finally, when there was a lull in the "conversation," I started backing toward the door and said, "So long, Mei Mei, see you tomorrow."

"Tomorrow!" Mei Mei repeated. "Yes, yes."

Well, I thought, while I practically galloped down the stairs, so that's what it feels like not to understand anything anyone is saying—poor Mei Mei.

Tuesday, September 11

At lunch today, Carla asked me if I was going to make it to practice this afternoon or if I had *babysitting* duty again. I didn't answer her immediately, and maybe I had an insulted expression on my face because she looked at me and said, "Uh-oh."

"I'm coming to soccer practice," I said, "and I'm bringing Mei Mei along."

The first problem was how to communicate my plans to Mei Mei and persuade her to come along. The second problem was how to let her family know that Mei Mei hadn't come home because she'd gone to the soccer field.

I consulted Mr. Spears again; he always knows how to solve a problem. He promised he'd call the Thompsons and make certain they conveyed the message to Mei Mei's family. Then I sat down at Mei Mei's table and drew her a picture like this while I was describing what we were going to do after school.

"Yes, yes—soccer," said Mei Mei, repeating after me.

I wasn't sure what would happen, but it's a free country, so if I wanted to bring Mei Mei to soccer, I was going to bring Mei Mei to soccer.

After school, Mei Mei and I took the bus to Samuelson Field, where everybody was already running around yelling and laughing, balls flying through the air. I went over to the coach, carrying my bag, and introduced myself.

"Today's an informal try-out," said the coach, flipping some pages on her clipboard. "You'd better hurry and get your things on."

"I've brought a friend who..."

The coach, whose name was Mariana, gave Mei Mei a quick look. "I can't let you play today," she told Mei Mei, "because you don't have any equipment, but you can do the opening workout with us today, then come back tomorrow with equipment and demonstrate what you can do. Have you played much?"

Mei Mei looked back at the coach with a totally lost expression, and I knew that she hadn't understood a word Mariana had said.

"I don't think so," I said.

By now the whole team was running circuits around the field, so we sneaked in at the back of the pack. Mei Mei kept up well; I was surprised but happy, because that's one of the critical parts of conditioning for soccer—it's absolutely necessary to have the stamina to keep running.

After the drills, I escorted Mei Mei over to a bench and said, "You sit here and watch for a while, OK?"

"OK, yes," she said, looking painfully uncertain—or was that disappointment I saw in her expression?

I went back in, and once I was warmed up, I really got into it. We divided up into teams and had a scrimmage, during which Mariana kept yelling at us to be aggressive, so I decided to be very aggressive and go all out for the ball.

"What's gotten into you?" Carla asked me admiringly.

I even scored two goals.

Mei Mei sat there alone on the bench looking as though she wanted to run out and join us—which really surprised me—and she applauded every time anyone made a good move, as if she really understood the game—which surprised me even more.

Practice ended, and the whole team was hooting and carrying on with excess exuberance—the way they always do the first day back. "If only she spoke English," Carla said to me, right in front of Mei Mei.

"She should find a learn-to-play-soccer team," said Betsy Olsen, trying to be considerate, I guess.

Parents in minivans began carrying off loads of girls, and Mariana told us good-bye and trotted off to her car.

"Come on, let's kick a ball around," I told Mei Mei, trying to be nice, "come on."

Mei Mei raced over; I took my ball, and we went out onto the field. I estimated we had fifteen minutes before the next team arrived and claimed it. I put the ball down, ran up to it, and gave it a deliberate, directed kick, much harder than I'd intended, toward Mei Mei. She stopped it with her foot—easily—and then centered herself behind the ball, took a few steps back, charged up to it, and kicked the ball like a maniac. It went at least 40 yards.

"Way to go, Mei Mei," I yelled at her.

I ran to the other end of the field to get the ball, motioned for her to follow me, and said, "Kick it again."

This time, she really booted it, an amazing feat for someone as slight as she is. Most power kickers tend to be tall and hefty, but Mei Mei kicked it farther than anyone I'd seen in a long time. "So you know how to play soccer," I said, smiling.

I'm positive she understood the significance of what I'd just said because she not only said, "Yes, yes, soccer, I play" but she gave me the most tremendous grin.

I smiled back and felt better than I'd felt in ages; my New-School-Year Resolution was working out better—much better—than I'd ever expected.

Wednesday, September 12

I loaned Mei Mei some equipment and took her to practice again today. I told Coach Mariana all about how Mei Mei was a wonderful soccer player. I was sure Mei Mei would create a sensation on the field, especially when we practiced goal kicks, and sure enough, she let loose with an incredibly powerful kick. The other girls' mouths dropped open a mile, and they all clapped and patted her on the back. Half of us put on pinnies, and we divided into two teams for a scrimmage. All through practice, everyone took to pantomiming and speaking slowly and simply, just to make sure Mei Mei was a part of the whole thing.

Monday, September 17

During recess on Thursday and Friday, and all weekend, Megan, Carla, and I practiced soccer with Mei Mei—who was just as good as everybody else, if not better.

Today at the end of practice, Mariana handed out our new team jerseys, which are purple with white numbers—I'm 26, and Mei Mei is 55. Then we all huddled to holler out a team cheer—"Tigers, *go wild!*"—and as the last syllables echoed off the bleachers, you could hear Mei Mei chirp, "Yes, yes, Tigers go wild!"

Tomorrow's our first game. With several new friends, including Mei Mei, and the potential for a great soccer season, I think seventh grade may turn out to be a great year!